1981

Sarah Winek

Presentation by *BookLeaf Publishing*

Web: www.bookleafpub.com

E-mail: info@bookleafpub.com

ISBN: 9789358736960

First edition 2023

*For Petey, Ella, Luca and Charlie - you all
have my heart, for always x*

ACKNOWLEDGEMENT

I would first like to acknowledge Christina Rossetti (1830 - 1894). She was the first poet that made me fall in love with poetry as a young 16-year-old girl, holed up in her bedroom reading. Her poem "Remember Me" made me contemplate rhyme and inspired me to play around with prose. In doing so, I found I was able to lexically experiment with my life experience to create 'art'.

I would also love to (most importantly!) acknowledge my beloved Husband, Christopher Winek - I love you! and also my three miracles - my children, Ella, Luca & Charlie - who are my absolute world. Thank you to my wonderful friends, particularly to Caroline; for being a truly beautiful human, for all of the obscenely early morning dog walks together, putting the world to rights and appreciating the sunrise at 6 am. Michelle - thank you for being my biggest writing champion - and for always believing in me as a 'good' writer. (Believers are everything!) Thank you also to Katie, Chantelle, Emma, Laura and Molly for our treasured friendship, for all the love, support and laughs that keep me sane along the way. To all those who didn't support my journey as a writer - thank you for the inspiration and the growth! I've learned not everyone will like you especially when you are authentic - and that's OK! It's life. Thank you also to my amazing writing group in Abu Dhabi - Andy, Eneida and Camilla - for all of your support and advice during my Middle Eastern chapter, editing and feedback at Fanr (and laughs) I love you talented people! Another huge thank you and shower of gratitude to BookLeaf Publishing for making this book even a possibility.

Lastly - Thank you to my grandparents - Barry & Dorothy Gough. Since 1981 for all of your love, for everything you gave and did. I love you.

PREFACE

1981 is my first collection of poetry. I have written about the 'ordinary' emotions life evokes through my poems. Themes that inspire me often depict the wild rollercoaster that is falling in (and out!) of love - then the magic of finding it again. Loss, questioning what it means to love and lose people, throughout the chapters of our lives is something we can all understand. We all have words unsaid, feelings that get buried and can instantly relate to one another through our shared experience of life. Love, death, joy, loss and grief unite us and mend the bonds that bind the fragility of our (often) messy human relationships.

Each poem reflects a little piece of my journey. A snapshot in verse of the people I have met, and the experiences I have had so far, living on our magnificently beautiful planet. Enjoy x

The Lighthouse

The lighthouse on the cliffs
You are the place that beckons me home
When my heart is disillusioned
and I am all alone.

I see the brightness of your love
A beautiful beacon, breaking through the black
Each ray a golden smile that calls to me
Telling me "come back"

Back to your heavenly arms, back to the velvet
of your kiss
Returning to my home again
Our private revelry is bliss

You're a wonder in white
Bracing ships adrift the bay
A thousand winds will curse you
Many others wouldn't stay

So, when the darkening skies surround you
and the tide's voice becomes too harsh
Let me be your lighthouse too
Together at last

Tongues

Tongues talk about you with vinegar-laced tips
But still, I love you.
Tongues talk and say you are a fool
But still, my blind heart defends you

Tongues talk and say you are plain
They lie! The only time I feel alive
is when I think upon the contours of your face.
Tongues talk and say you are a Tyrant

Tongues talk, they slay you straight through
Slanderous and sly
Yet, even after all their protests
I still protect you

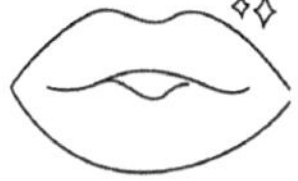

So Well

I don't know where I am going
I just know where I have been
I don't know who I shall love
I just know those in-between
I anticipate the sunrise
Then, I sit. I reflect.
On the silvery moon that fell
Across the liquorice sky
So happy I've felt so far today
So happy, and so well

If I Should Die Tonight

If I should die tonight
Dress me in the dark
Put on my sequin dress and silver sandals
Take me to the park

Crack open a bottle of the best Champagne
Prop me up on a bench
Together we can toast Cassiopeia
Her beauty is immense

People will stare and think you are mad!
If they do - ignore them
Caress my decaying hand
Whisper softly our secrets
Tell me you understand

I'll be still and you'll be warm
I shall grow colder by the hour
Skin like porcelain, bones grow stiff
Lift me up in your arms and
Carry me

Lay me down where you proposed
Wrap me up now, nice and tight
Kiss me my darling
Bid me adieu and goodnight!

He's the Devil

He's already under my skin
Yet he's just walked through the door
I don't want to give in
But I've been here before

Why is sin so intoxicating?
My virtue falls to the floor
I don't want to give in
But he's demanding much more

He outwits me quick
Keeps me guessing … and yet
I can't stop thinking about him
Jesus wept! We've just met

He's so wrong to the core
This love affair will drive me mad
I let him pour me another one
Finest whisky (on tab)

He's the Devil and he knows it
Licks his lips. I have to go home
But at the same time I'm agreeing
"Ok, one more for the road"

Heartache

My heart aches
Like you've just left
In reality, it's been an age
My heart drums your name without rest

I'm a shell of a person. I'm a ghost in the crowd
Swallowed like an oyster by the ocean
There's a question in my head
Did you care that we met?

Beat

Beat me to the finish line
Take me out of the race
My heart can't help but underline
The memory of your face

Beat me to the end of the road
Race me until we are done
Since we started, I've lost myself
You know that you have won

Swifts

Swifts swoop all summer long
They carry the seeds of my heart
Scattered over downs, that gleam with rapeseed
Billowing in the wind like baskets of gold

Parts of my love remain there still
Buried in the dry ground
Flickering under the red bellies of worms
Slinking slowly without purpose

Parts of my love, swifts have abandoned
At the foot of England's white cliffs
Never to be seen again
Forever lost under her shores

Parts of my love have blown adrift
The swifts have lost them now
Obscured by the desert sun
Lost forevermore.

Blackjack

Life is a game of dice
That's what life can be
Roll three to win, roll two for me
Roll a straight seven and get through the pain
Roll a double baby
You have to start over again

Then. There is Blackjack.
He sneaks up on you slow
You never see him coming
How far will you let him go?
He will take you to the end
He will bleed you
Watch you obsess
Steal all your chips and all of your joy
Make you believe you are worthless
and deserve nothing more
'Wake up' he cries
'Play again' he might say
Watch out when the odds are just too good
Blackjack's coming your way

I Let Go

I loosen my tongue in my mouth
It's tightly coiled around your name
My jaw, tense and unflinching
I breathe and let go

My ears are eager for your words
I blink slowly and decide to rest
My shoulders have risen and stiffened
I breathe and let go

I send you love
With all my heart and good intentions
I send some to myself
Then, I breathe and let go

Happy

Happy is a word I treasure
It says so much, with five lovely letters
H-A-P-P-Y
Each one carries unspoken pressure
How happy are you?

Everyone chases it
Some find it. Many pretend
Happy. How do we measure?
I smile only because I know.
It's being alive.
It's now.

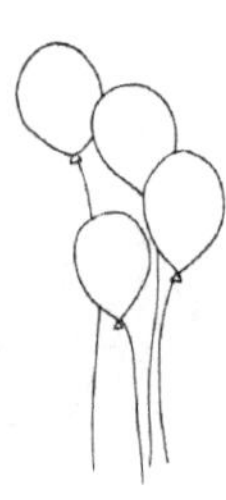

Drowning From The Inside

The black water swells at my throat
Rushing around the tender skin that covers my
body
I feel the wind change and I. Stop!
Paralysed by this rising darkness that
consumes me from the inside
I can't go over it, I can't go under it
I drown from the inside

Lungs are the last to fill. Breath fails
Brain is on fire
Depression ravages each synapse, each brain cell
flushes from healthy pink to ash
The past. The present. The future
All swallowed by my monstrous mental illness
I close my eyes
I drown from the inside

Summer Rain

It falls soft as an angel's whisper
Cutting through the hot blanket of a summer
in June
Summer rain

My senses summoned to life by heaven's kiss
My neck shimmers wet against it
Summer rain

The solemn clouds rumble with the weight of
water
The heaviness makes them sag, settle heavy
Mirroring the ground
Summer rain

Let it not be the Lark

Let it not be the Lark
That calls outside my window
If it is, then the day is truly over
You are no longer mine

Let it be the Nightingale
That sings its sweet melancholy song
Binding our bodies in the night
With notes of sweet honey and apple dew

Don't let that Lark sit on my ledge
Telling me our hour is up
My bittersweet memory of your voice
Etched into my mind like neon graffiti

Your eyes burn into mine and
for a moment
I am lost. Lost to time
You are a stranger to me now

It is the Lark
Sorrow breaks the day with the unwanted song
of this unlucky bird
I have to let you go

My Empty Cradle

I lie here and feel numb
Sad for a life that had just begun
and yet - it's over.
Gone

My body was a life vessel
Mother's haven in which
you could grow.
Now it's just an empty cradle.

My pulse races and my heart aches
I just want you to fill me up,
The space you left - a hollow reminder
Of a life that can't be replaced.

A minute heart that beat
with sweet potential and yet -
Beats, no more.
Is no more.

My empty cradle
My body is hostage to your departure
Please, I beg the silence
Don't let my baby go.

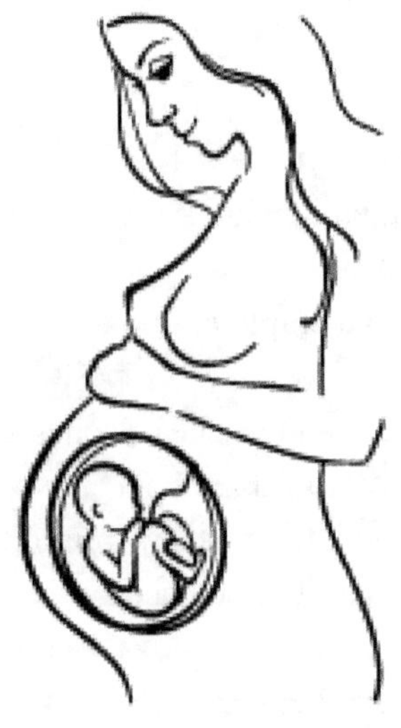

A Mother's Grief

A mother's grief knows no limit
It rises with the sun and outlasts the moon
Fiercely illuminating
the barren shores of her heart

A crimson purse; now frozen and hard
Like a splintered diamond in her chest
Grief flows through her veins like hot molten
metal
She bides her time

The noisy days of her life pass
Clocks tick down until the day
She can be reunited, without empty silence
Hold her departed young once again

Black Dog

The black dog is here again
I hear him
Panting by my side
The black dog knows it's time again
Time for me to sink down with him, into the
shadows
My tired back slides
Down the hostile wall of doom
No warning today. No warning at all
He paralyses me, the black dog

I don't always see him coming
He's always there though.
Waiting, by the door
Around the corners of my memory
Looking at me intently with his white eyes
Watching and waiting
I slump and curl into my body, trying to hide
I can't make him go.

Just the black dog and me
Two's company
But his company
Makes me feel so alone

Fleeting Love

Love is fleeting
Love is what we will leave behind us
When all of our golden days are gone
The laughter of our life
will echo in forgotten alleyways
Kisses will go on, pass to another and another
and on
Quick! Like the click of a key
On a summer evening, late at night
Love is all there is
Years roll by so fast
Told through the lips of the living
To the tombs of our beloved dead
Romantic remains of the past

Beautiful Otherness

Beautiful otherness
Evanescent love of our youth
And yet, the echo keeps me wondering
Twisting our truth

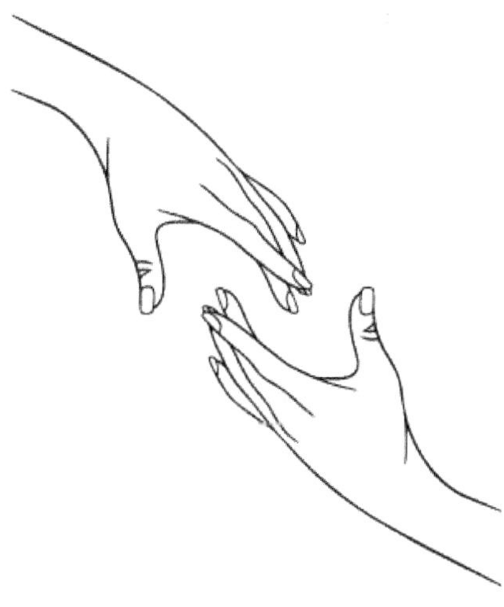

Fate

You're so over the top and under my skin
This beat of our love has no beginning
Skin moist. Tongues kiss
Bodies sick with lust

I don't want to forget it
but forget it, I must.
You seduced me softly, and then
whipped me with words

The day we collided
A blessing or curse?
Tonight, the skies are easy.
Tiresias predicted you would leave

I lay under the stars
Who listen as my pride wails,
You stole my heart -
from my sleeve.

Big Love

You are my big love
Tall, beautifully ernest you
Like a hurricane, you blow everyone else away
without even trying to

You are my big love
I'm blessed to the core
I know I've met my match
Fate has settled the score

You are truly my big love
Fill me up - and then
Tell me, how I am Helen of Troy
Crooked smile me once again

Seasons fly and you become my greyer love
more distinguished by time
Let's stay together, stop the tick of the clock
I'm yours forever